LORENA PAJALUNGA

Good Morning Yoga

Relaxing Poses for Children

ILLUSTRATIONS BY ANNA LÁNG

WSkids
WHITE STAR KIDS

GOOD MORNING YOGA

The word YOGA comes from the Sanskrit root *yuj*, which means "bind togeth-er", "UNITE" or "hold fast". Therefore, by binding and connecting while doing yoga, we can reunite all opposites harmoniously: body and mind; individual and universe; head and heart; respiration and sensations; psyche and memory; activity and passivity; desire and abandonment.

The classical yoga of Patanjali is a path, a methodology and a philosophy, in which "ASANAS" – the poses – are just a small part of the journey towards self-realization, which has various names depending on different cultures and traditions. THE POSES ARE IN FACT THE PERFECT WAY FOR US TO SPARK CHILDREN'S INTEREST AND BRING THEM CLOSER TO THE WORLD OF YOGA, making it possible to transmit

the important lessons and values that this ancient discipline has handed down over millennia. Experience has taught me that CHILDREN ALWAYS POSSESS AND SHOW AN EXTRAORDINARY ABILITY to go be-yond the physicality and practicality of asanas: they are able to immediately and instinctively grasp the energetic and symbolic aspects that the poses teach us, allowing the true essence of yoga to emerge effortlessly.

This is why it is important to encourage children to practice yoga, especially in the morning. This discipline is perfect for helping them to WAKE UP AND PREPARE THEMSELVES FOR THE DAY AHEAD, LEAVING THEM FULL OF ENERGY AND POSITIVITY, WITH AN AMAZING SENSE OF CALM AND CONFIDENCE.

The sequence in the book is made up of poses and practices to reawaken their energy, helping them to feel THE WONDERFULNESS OF THE BEGINNING OF A NEW DAY, in harmony with nature, friends and the entire universe.

By nature, children have AN INEXHAUSTIBLE SOURCE OF ENERGY, and this is why parents, grandparents, teachers, and all those involved in their education, have the difficult task of teaching them how to best convey and channel it, and not, as we often mistakenly think, "vent" it.

Thanks to the symbolic and energetic value of the poses we have selected, YOGA CAN BE A UNIQUE TOOL FOR US TO "PLAY" WITH CHILDREN IN THIS DIRECTION.

Teaching yoga to children from an early age is like planting a seed in extremely fertile soil, with the knowledge that, over the years, precious qualities such as determination, calmness, empathy and concentration will spontaneously emerge in them.

IT'S TIME TO WAKE UP!

A slender, timid ray of sunshine filters through the window and lights up the room. It's still early, but Anna opens her eyes and looks around. She yawns happily: she feels rested and full of energy. The first thing she does, is to go over to her little brother's bed: "Teo, it's morning! It's time to wake up!"

The little boy rubs his eyes and smiles: "Let's go and wake Mom and Dad up!"

"Why don't we play with our cuddly toys a bit first? We had lots fun playing with them yesterday evening before going to sleep, didn't we?"

"Loads!" agrees Teo, nodding his head enthusiastically. "I felt really calm and peaceful after playing with them; and I fell asleep immediately! But I'm not tired now! I want to skip, play, run, dance, and…"

"So do we!", says a small voice, "We certainly don't want to spend all day sitting still on a shelf!"

The two children aren't at all afraid when they see it is Anna's cuddly hedgehog who has spoken. Their toys always come to life when they play make-believe games: they talk, laugh and move around, just like them. There really isn't anything strange about it at all!

"It's impossible for us to stay still once we've woken up!", adds Teo's crocodile. "It's an amazing feeling; but we know how to make it even better. We all have a secret, a particular pose; a little magic that — if it's done right — will transform our morning energy into strength and fun for the whole day!"

"Anna, come over here," says the hedgehog,

"You and I will start!"

The
ROCKING-CHAIR Pose

ROCKING & ROLLING

COME AND SIT NEXT TO ME. NOW, CROSS YOUR LEGS AND ANKLES, HOLD YOUR TOES AND EXHALE, CURLING YOUR BACK FORWARDS AND ROUNDING IT AS MUCH AS POSSIBLE; LIKE I'M DOING. NOW WE'RE GOING TO ROCK BACKWARDS AND FORWARDS LIKE A ROCKING CHAIR.

1

Sit with your legs crossed, put your hands over your crossed ankles, and hold your toes.

2

Around your back as much as possible.

3

Very slowly, roll down onto your back, keeping it curved, and rock up and down.

This pose showed me how to have fun with my body.

The
PALM TREE Pose

TALA-ASANA

THIS POSE WILL MAKE YOU FEEL REALLY TALL! LET'S TRY IT TOGETHER! COME AND STAND NEXT TO ME, WITH YOUR LEGS SLIGHTLY APART. LET'S CHOOSE A FIXED POINT IN FRONT OF US TO LOOK AT: THIS WILL HELP US TO CONCENTRATE AND KEEP OUR BALANCE. NOW WE INHALE AND OPEN OUR ARMS OUT TO THE SIDES, LIFTING THEM UNTIL THEY ARE POINTING TOWARDS THE SKY, WITH THE ELBOWS AND FINGERS STRAIGHT AND THE PALMS OF OUR HANDS FACING EACH OTHER. EXHALING, WE GO UP ONTO THE TIPS OF OUR TOES, TRYING TO KEEP OUR BALANCE FOR AS LONG AS POSSIBLE.

1

Stand with your feet slightly apart and concentrate on a fixed point in front of you.

2

Inhale and extend your arms up towards the sky.

3

Exhale and go up onto the tips of your toes; try to keep your balance for as long as possible.

In this pose, I feel like a really tall palm tree being kissed by the sun!

ENERGY
Charge

SHAKTI-SHOWER

I FIND IT IMPOSSIBLE TO STAY STILL; WHAT ABOUT YOU? THEN LET'S NOT STAY STILL TOGETHER! LET'S START BY MASSAGING OUR HEAD AND FACE WITH OUR HANDS. NOW WE'RE GOING TO GENTLY TAP OUR WHOLE BODY WITH OUR FINGERTIPS, AS IF THEY WERE LOTS OF TINY RAINDROPS. CAN YOU FEEL YOUR ENERGY COMING BACK AFTER BEING ASLEEP ALL NIGHT?

1
Massage your head
and face with your hands,
very gently.

2
Tap your fingers across
your chest, along your arms
and down your back.

3
Continue down your legs
and onto the soles
of your feet.

With this pose, I learned how to reawaken my whole body, from the tips of my toes to the top of my head!

SUN
Salutation

WATCH THE SUNLIGHT COMING THROUGH THE WINDOW: ITS GOLDEN RAYS WARM THE EARTH AND CHASE AWAY THE DARKNESS OF THE NIGHT, AWAKENING PEOPLE, ANIMALS AND PLANTS. NOTHING TRANSMITS MORE ENERGY THAN THE SUN! THIS IS WHY I LOVE TO GREET IT EVERY MORNING WITH POSES AND SPECIAL WORDS: REPEAT AFTER ME!

1. Here I am
2. I'm a ray of sunshine
3. I bow to greet the earth
4. I'm ready
5. I bring light to the mountains
6. To the animals
7. To nature
8. I give warmth to the earth
9. I listen to myself
10. I respect myself
11. I'm happy
12. And in peace

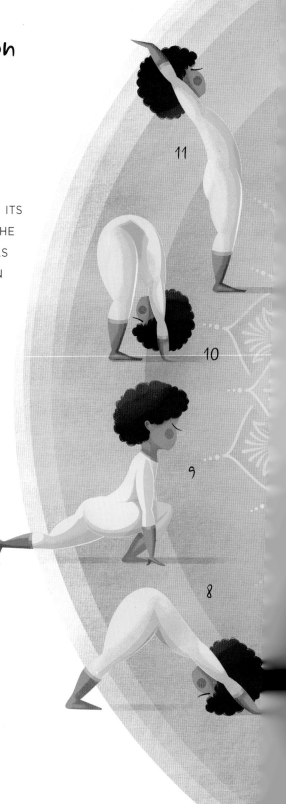

The TREE
Pose

___

VRKS-ASANA

COME AND STAND NEXT TO ME. LET'S CHOOSE A FIXED POINT IN FRONT OF US TO LOOK AT: IT WILL HELP US KEEP OUR BALANCE! NOW, SHIFT THE WEIGHT OF YOUR BODY ONTO YOUR LEFT LEG AND LIFT YOUR RIGHT FOOT OFF THE GROUND. PLACE THE SOLE OF YOUR FOOT ON THE INSIDE OF YOUR LEFT THIGH; LIKE I'M DOING. WHEN YOU FEEL STEADY, SLOWLY PUT THE PALMS OF YOUR HANDS TOGETHER IN FRONT OF YOUR CHEST, THEN SLOWLY LIFT YOUR ARMS ABOVE YOUR HEAD, AS IF YOUR HANDS AND ARMS WERE THE CROWN OF A TREE AND YOUR FEET THE ROOTS.

1
Standing, choose a fixed point to look at to help you keep your balance.

2
Shift your weight onto your left leg and lift your right foot off the ground. Then place it on your left thigh.

3
Put the palms of your hands together in front of your chest and lift your arms above your head.

I learned the importance of having deep roots, which help me keep my balance, even when I'm hyperactive.

The PEACEFUL WARRIOR 1 Pose

VIRABHADRA-ASANA 1

WE'RE GOING TO SHOW YOU THREE PEACEFUL WARRIOR POSES: I'LL START!

WE'RE GOING TO START BY STANDING WITH OUR LEGS WIDE APART AND OUR ARMS OPEN. NOW WE TURN OUR RIGHT FOOT OUTWARDS AND BEND THE KNEE TO A NINETY-DEGREE ANGLE. WE PUT THE PALMS OF OUR HANDS TOGETHER ABOVE OUR HEAD AND FOLLOW OUR HANDS WITH OUR EYES. NOW REPEAT ON THE LEFT SIDE.

1

Standing, spread your legs wide apart and open your arms at shoulder height.

2

Turn your right foot outwards towards the knee, aligning it with your ankle.

3

Put the palms of your hands together, pointing them and your eyes towards the sky. Repeat on the other side.

I now understand that even the most courageous warrior must be able to concentrate.

The PEACEFUL WARRIOR 2 Pose

VIRABHADRA-ASANA 2

WE START FROM THE WARRIOR 1 POSE THAT THE FLAMINGO SHOWED YOU. WE FOLLOW OUR RIGHT HAND WITH OUR EYES UNTIL WE'RE LOOKING AT THE PALM, WHICH IS TURNED UPWARDS. I HAVE THIN LEGS, BUT THEY FEEL STRONG IN THIS POSE!
NOW REPEAT THE MOVEMENTS ON THE OTHER SIDE.

1
Standing, spread your legs wide apart and open your arms at shoulder height.

2
Turn your right foot outwards towards the knee, aligning it with your ankle.

3
Turn your head to look at your right hand, keeping your palm facing upwards.

This pose evokes the strength of a warrior, with which to face the day ahead.

The PEACEFUL WARRIOR 3 Pose

VIRABHADRA-ASANA 3

PUT YOURSELF IN THE WARRIOR 2 POSE THAT THE MOUSE TAUGHT YOU: WELL DONE! WE SHIFT OUR WEIGHT ONTO THE FRONT LEG, FULLY EXTENDING IT; NOW WE BEND OUR ARMS, HEAD AND TORSO FORWARDS UNTIL THE ENTIRE UPPER PART OF OUR BODY IS PARALLEL TO THE GROUND. AT THE SAME TIME, WE LIFT THE BACK LEG, WHICH SHOULD ALSO BE EXTENDED, CREATING A SINGLE LINE WITH THE REST OF OUR BODY. ALL CLEAR? GOOD. NOW LET'S REPEAT THE POSE ON THE OTHER SIDE.

1
Shift your weight onto the front leg and straighten your knee.

2
Bend your torso, stretched-out arms and head forwards, until they are parallel to the ground.

3
Straighten the back leg so that your entire body is aligned in a single imaginary line.

In this pose, I can feel the energy leaving my body so that I can share it with my friends.

The DANCING SHIVA Pose

NATARAJA SHIVA-ASANA

COME AND STAND NEXT TO ME. WE SHIFT OUR WEIGHT ONTO THE LEFT LEG, LIFT OUR RIGHT FOOT TOWARDS OUR BUTTOCK AND HOLD THE BACK OF OUR FOOT WITH THE RIGHT HAND. WITH OUR LEFT HAND, WE DO A HAND GESTURE CALLED "CIN MUDRA": THIS IS A VERY POWERFUL SYMBOL THAT KEEPS OUR ENERGY FROM FLOWING. AND IT'S REALLY EASY TO DO! LOOK AT MY FEATHERS AND DO THE SAME THING WITH YOUR FINGERS. NOW WE BEND OUR TORSO FORWARDS SLIGHTLY, MOVE OUR HEEL AWAY FROM THE BUTTOCK AND ARCH OUR BACK. FINALLY, WE LIFT OUR ARM UP AS IF IT WERE AN ARROW BEING FIRED BY THE BOW OF OUR BODY.

1

Balancing on your right foot, bring your right heel up to your buttock and hold the back of your foot with the right hand.

2

Make the cin mudra symbol with your left hand, while stretching your arm forwards and upwards.

3

Bend forwards slightly, arching your back, and move your heel away from your buttock.

The Toucan taught me the value and strength of even the smallest gesture.

The LIGHTNING BOLT Pose

VAJR-ASANA

NOW, COME HERE AND SIT ON YOUR HEELS: I BET YOU'RE THINKING THAT THIS IS A REALLY BORING POSE. BUT IF YOU COPY WHAT I DO, YOU'LL TURN INTO A FIERY LIGHTNING BOLT IN JUST A FEW SECONDS! WE SIT UP ON OUR KNEES AND PUSH OUR PELVIS FORWARDS; THEN WE ALIGN OUR BACK. INHALING, WE STRETCH OUR ARMS OUT IN FRONT OF US, IN LINE WITH THE SHOULDERS, WITH OUR FINGERS STRETCHED OUT. WE EXHALE AND DRAW THE LETTER Z WITH OUR BODY BY BENDING OUR HEAD, TORSO AND THIGHS BACKWARDS, KEEPING EVERYTHING ALIGNED. CAN YOU FEEL THE LIGHTNING ENERGY FLOWING THROUGH YOUR BODY?

1
Start by sitting on your heels, then sit up on your knees and push your pelvis forward.

2
Inhale, align your back and stretch out your arms.

3
Exhale and bend your head, torso and thighs backwards, drawing the letter Z with your body.

This pose teaches me to be light and fresh, like the air we breathe after a spring storm.

The PIGEON
Pose

KAPOTA-ASANA

MY POSE REQUIRES A LITTLE BIT OF BALANCE: SIT ON YOUR KNEES AND PUT YOUR RIGHT FOOT FORWARDS. SHIFT ALL OF YOUR WEIGHT FORWARDS, GOING DOWN INTO A LUNGE WITH YOUR RIGHT LEG AND STRETCHING YOUR LEFT LEG OUT BEHIND YOU. NOW PUT YOUR RIGHT HAND ONTO YOUR THIGH AND TURN YOUR HEAD BACKWARDS, AT THE SAME TRYING TO GRAB THE BACK OF YOUR LEFT FOOT WITH YOUR LEFT HAND. PULL YOUR FOOT TOWARDS YOU, WITHOUT LOSING YOUR BALANCE! CONCENTRATE ON A FIXED POINT TO HELP YOU STAY STEADY FOR LONGER. SHALL WE TRY IT THE OTHER SIDE?

1

Kneel on the ground
and put your right foot forwards,
lunging onto it with all your weight.

2

Turn your head backwards and take
the back of your left foot in your left hand;
pull it towards you while trying to keep your
balance. Now repeat on the other side.

Thanks to this pose, I feel like a bird singing at sunrise.

The ROOSTER
Pose

KUKKUT-ASANA

FINALLY, IT'S MY TURN! I'M GOING TO SHOW YOU A POSE THAT REQUIRES LOTS OF BALANCE AND ADMITTEDLY SEVERAL TRIES BEFORE YOU GET IT RIGHT; BUT ONCE YOU'VE GOT IT, YOU'LL FEEL FULL OF CONFIDENCE AND COURAGE! LET'S BEGIN! CROUCH ON THE FLOOR, WITH THE SOLES OF YOUR FEET PLANTED FIRMLY ON THE GROUND AND YOUR PELVIS RAISED. SPREAD YOUR FINGERS AND PUT YOUR HANDS ON THE FLOOR IN FRONT OF YOU, WITH YOUR ELBOWS BENT. SLOWLY SHIFT THE WEIGHT OF YOUR BODY FROM YOUR FEET TO YOUR HANDS, UNTIL YOUR KNEES TOUCH YOUR ELBOWS, OR UPPER ARMS... NOW, VERY GRADUALLY, LIFT ONE FOOT AT A TIME OFF THE FLOOR, UNTIL YOU ARE BALANCING ON YOUR HANDS!

1
Crouch down with your feet planted firmly on the ground and your pelvis raised off the floor.

2
Spread out your fingers and put your hands on the floor; start shifting your weight forwards, balancing yourself a bit.

3
Move your knees forwards, one at a time, until they touch your elbows or upper arms, balance on your hands while you lift your feet off the floor.

This pose fills me with courage and dispels all my fears and insecurities.

The RESTING WARRIOR
Pose

VIRASANA (VARIATION)

THAT ROOSTER'S POSE WAS REALLY ACROBATIC! MY FAVORITE IS MUCH EASIER, BUT IT'S PERFECT FOR GATHERING ENERGY! COME HERE AND I'LL SHOW YOU. WE SIT ON OUR HEELS AND POSITION OUR LEFT LEG SO THAT THE SOLE OF THE LEFT FOOT IS ON THE FLOOR, IN LINE WITH THE RIGHT KNEE. FINALLY, WE PLACE OUR LEFT ELBOW ON THE LEFT KNEE, WITH ONE HAND SUPPORTING OUR CHIN.

1

Sit on your heels with your back nice and straight.

2

Now move your left foot forwards so that it is in line with your right knee, which you're kneeling on.

3

Put your elbow on your knee and rest your chin on your left hand, which should be open to support the weight of your relaxed head.

The Piglet taught me that peace and silence allow me to listen to what is going on inside of me, so that I can find the same wonderfulness in the world.

The DIAMOND Pose

SUPTA VAJRA-ASANA

WAIT, DON'T GET UP! WE'RE GOING TO START FROM THE RESTING WARRIOR POSE TO DO AN EQUALLY VALUABLE ONE TO CONSERVE OUR ENERGY! WE TURN OUR HEELS OUTWARDS SO OUR BUTTOCKS TOUCH THE FLOOR. NOW WE PLACE OUR ELBOWS ON THE FLOOR AND ARCH BACKWARDS UNTIL THE TOP OF OUR HEAD TOUCHES THE GROUND, BENT BACKWARDS.

1

Sitting on your heels, turn your feet outwards so your buttocks are on the floor.

2

Put your elbows on the floor, arch your back and bend your head back until it's touching the ground. Concentrate on the center of your chest and imagine that you are breathing into your heart.

This pose teaches me to how to feel the shining jewel in my heart.

SAGE MARICHY'S
Pose

MARICHY-ASANA

YOU'VE ALREADY FELT LIKE A BOLT OF LIGHTNING, SO HOW WOULD YOU LIKE TO FEEL LIKE A TORNADO? THIS POSE WILL DO JUST THAT! SIT WITH YOUR LEGS STRETCHED OUT IN FRONT OF YOU. INHALE AND WHILE DOING SO BRING YOUR RIGHT KNEE UP AND PUT YOUR FOOT FLAT ON THE GROUND. NOW EXHALE AND OPEN YOUR ARMS LIKE THE WINGS OF A MAJESTIC BIRD. TURN YOUR TORSO TO THE RIGHT; PLACE THE TIP OF YOUR LEFT ELBOW ON THE OUTSIDE OF YOUR RIGHT KNEE AND BEND YOUR ARM, KEEPING THE PALM OF YOUR HAND OPEN. LOOK BACKWARDS, BEYOND THE HAND THAT IS ON THE FLOOR BEHIND YOU.

1
Sit with your legs stretched out in front of you. Put your right foot flat on the floor next to your left knee.

2
Exhale, open your arms and turn your torso to the right.

3
Place the tip of your left elbow on the outside of your right knee and put your right hand on the floor. Look behind you.

The Goat has helped me understand how to contain my strength in a spiral, with me at the center!

The HALF LOTUS
Pose
with namaskara mudra

ARDHA PADMA-ASANA WITH NAMASKARA MUDRA

THIS IS THE LAST POSE THAT WE'RE GOING TO SHOW YOU! SIT ON THE FLOOR WITH YOUR LEGS STRETCHED OUT; BEND YOUR RIGHT LEG AND PUT THE BACK OF YOUR FOOT ONTO YOUR LEFT INNER GROIN. BEND YOUR LEFT LEG UNDER THE RIGHT ONE. KEEPING YOUR BACK PERFECTLY STRAIGHT, PUT THE PALMS OF YOUR HANDS TOGETHER IN FRONT OF YOUR CHEST. THIS HAND GESTURE HAS A DIFFICULT NAME – NAMASKARA MUDRA – BUT IT'S VERY POWERFUL! PUSH YOUR PALMS TOGETHER, WITH YOUR ELBOWS OPEN WIDE.

1
Sit with your legs crossed
and your back nice
and straight.

2
Put your most flexible foot
onto the opposite inner groin,
leaving the other foot
where it is.

3
Put your hands in the
namaskara mudra position,
in front of your chest,
to express your gratitude
for the day to come.

Finally, after all that preparation, I feel ready to face the wonderful day that awaits me! Namaste!

GOOD MORNING
Yoga Sequence

Although this book is aimed at very young children, we would also like to convey to parents the idea that yoga poses are not just recreational; that each one is beneficial and associated with energetic qualities. For this to happen, however, the sequence must have a very precise structure: in fact, each pose has a meaning and an order that is not random and must therefore be respected. The Good Morning Yoga sequence in this book can be also practiced by adults, so they too can experience the benefits of doing it from start to finish.

1-Rocking-chair, 2-Palm Tree, 3-Energy Charge, 4-Sun Salutation, 5-Tree, 6-Peaceful Warrior 1, 7-Peaceful Warrior 2, 8-Peaceful Warrior 3, 9-Dancing Shiva, 10-Lightning Bolt, 11-Pigeon, 12-Rooster, 13-Resting Warrior, 14-Diamond, 15-Sage Marichy, 16-Half Lotus.

LORENA V. PAJALUNGA

(Swami Pragya Chaksu Saraswati) was given the task of teaching yoga to children thirty years ago by Swami Satyananda, her teacher at the Bihar School of Yoga in Munger, India. She therefore founded the Italian Children's Yoga Association (AIYB), which then became a First-level Master's degree program offered by the Faculty of Educational Sciences at Suor Orsola Benincasa University in Naples. She has a degree in Educational Sciences and teaches yoga at the "GiocaYoga®" workshop that is part of the Pedagogy of the Body course at the Bicocca University in Milan. In recent years, she has written a number of books for White Star Kids including for this series "Play Yoga, Have Fun and Grow Healthy and Happy!" and "Good Night Yoga, Relaxing Bedtime Poses for Children".

ANNA LÁNG

Is a Hungarian graphic designer and illustrator who currently lives and works in Milan. After getting her degree in graphic design from the Hungarian University of Fine Arts in Budapest in 2011, she worked for an advertising agency for three years. During the same period, she worked with the National Theater in Budapest, and in 2013 she received the Békéscsaba city award at the Hungarian Graphic Design Biennial, for her Shakespeare Poster Series. Today she illustrates children's books, which she does with great passion. In recent years she has brilliantly illustrated a number of titles for White Star Kids, including, for this series, "Play Yoga, Have Fun and Grow Healthy and Happy!" and "Good Night Yoga, Relaxing Bedtime Poses for Children".

WSkids
WHITE STAR KIDS

White Star Kids® is a registered trademark property of White Star s.r.l.

© 2018 White Star s.r.l.
Piazzale Luigi Cadorna, 6 - 20123 Milan, Italy
www.whitestar.it

Translation and Editing: TperTradurre s.r.l., Rome

ISBN 978-88-544-1295-8
1 2 3 4 5 6   22 21 20 19 18

Printed in Italy by Rotolito S.p.A. - Seggiano di Pioltello (MI)